Question Time

EXPLORE AND DISCOVER

Mammals

Jim Bruce

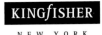

KING*fisher*

NEW YORK

Editor: Emma Wild
Designer: Catherine Goldsmith
DTP Coordinator: Nicky Studdart
Consultants: Joyce Pope, Norah Granger
Indexer: Sue Lightfoot
Production controllers: Jacquie Horner, Caroline Hansell
Illustrators: Ruth Lindsay 8–9, 14–15, 22–23; **Lisa Alderson** 12–13, 18–19; **Robin Budden** 26–27.
Cartoons: Ian Dicks
Picture Manager: Jane Lambert
Picture acknowledgments: 7*cr* Ingrid N.Visser/Planet Earth Pictures; 9*cl* Michael Gogden/www.osf.uk.com; 17*tl* Fritz Polking/Still Pictures; 21*tr* E A Janes/RSPCA Photo library; 27*cr* Images Colour Library.

Every effort has been made to trace the copyright holders of the photographs. The publishers apologize for any inconvenience caused.

KINGFISHER
Larousse Kingfisher Chambers Inc.
95 Madison Avenue
New York, New York 10016
www.lkcpub.com

First published in 2001
10 9 8 7 6 5 4 3 2 1

1TR/1200/TIM/RNB/MA128

LIBRARY OF CONGRESS
CATALOGING–IN–PUBLICATION DATA
has been applied for.

ISBN 0-7534-5340-1 (HC)
ISBN 0-7534-5408-4 (PB)

Printed in China

CONTENTS

ABOUT this book

Have you ever wondered what a kangaroo has in its pouch? Have all your questions about mammals answered, and learn other fascinating facts on every information-packed page of this book. Words in **bold** are defined in the glossary on page 31.

Look and find ★ dragonfly

All through the book you will see the **Look and find** symbol. This has the name and picture of a small object that is hidden somewhere on the page. Look carefully, and see if you can find it.

Now I know . . .

★ These boxes contain quick answers to all of the questions.
★ They will help you remember all about the amazing world of mammals.

WHAT is a mammal?

Although mice, bats, giraffes, leopards, and whales may seem very different, they all belong to a group of animals called mammals. Mammals are animals that have special things in common. They are **warm-blooded**, have fur or body hair, and have bony skeletons that support their bodies. Most mammals give birth to live young, and the mothers feed their young on their milk. All these things are true about us, so humans are mammals, too.

Giraffes feeding and drinking

Mother leopard with cub

HOW many kinds of mammals are there?

There are at least 4,300 different **species**, or kinds, of mammals. Sometimes, a new species of mammal is discovered, but there are probably no more than a few new species left to be found.

Field mouse

That's amazing!

Humans live longer than any other mammal—a few people have lived past their 120th birthdays!

Mammals are the most intelligent of all the animals and have extra-large brains!

4

HOW big do mammals grow?

Mammals come in all shapes and sizes—from miniscule to monstrous. About half of all known mammals are small **rodents**, such as squirrels and mice, and about one fourth are bats. Some mammals, such as elephants, whales, and lions, grow to be very large. Found in the ocean, the blue whale is the biggest mammal of all—it weighs more than 150 tons. The largest land mammal is the African elephant, which can weigh up to eight tons.

Although human babies are bigger than many fully grown mammals, they are completely helpless. They need their parents to look after them for many years.

Now I know . . .

★ Mammals look different, but they have many characteristics in common.

★ More than 4,300 different species of mammals exist.

★ Some mammals grow to be very large, but many are small.

5

HOW do polar bears keep warm?

Like all mammals, polar bears are warm-blooded. Their bodies stay at the same temperature whether the air or water around them is hot or cold. Most mammals are also covered in hair. Polar bears have a thick coat to protect them from the freezing cold of the **arctic**. In the winter they find shelter in a **den**, a hole that they dig in the snow.

WHY is a polar bear white?

As well as keeping it warm, a polar bear's thick, white coat helps **camouflage** it against the snow when it hunts for food. In fact, its whole body is perfect for life in its surroundings. Its large paws are excellent snowshoes, as well as great paddles for swimming.

That's amazing!

Polar bears do not need to drink. They get all their fluids from the food they eat!

Polar bears can swim 62 miles (100km) without stopping!

Polar bear

6

WHAT makes a walrus fat?

Under its skin a walrus has a thick layer of fat called **blubber**. This keeps it warm in the icy waters of the Arctic Ocean. Other arctic mammals, such as polar bears and seals, also have this layer of fat to protect them from the cold. A walrus has two long, sharp tusks, which it uses to dig up shellfish and crabs from the seabed. Its tusks are also used as weapons when fighting.

Seal

To stay fat and warm, arctic mammals have to eat a lot of food. A polar bear eats seals, fish, seabirds, and walruses, plus plants and berries in the summer. Polar bears have an amazing sense of smell. They can sniff out a live seal over 3 feet (1m) under the ice.

Now I know . . .

★ All mammals are warm-blooded.

★ A polar bear's white coat camouflages it against the snow.

★ Blubber is a layer of fat under arctic mammals' skin that keeps them warm.

WHERE do mammals live?

Mammals live almost everywhere in the world—in water as well as on land. Every kind of mammal has its own **habitat**. This is the place where it finds its food and spends most of its life. Mammals are found in places as different as dry deserts, wet forests, hot tropics, and even freezing polar regions.

WHAT does a camel have in its hump?

Camels are well equipped for life in the hot, dry desert. They can survive for days without food and water. The humps on their backs store a large amount of fat, which provides energy for them when they cannot find food.

Dromedary camels have one hump

That's amazing!

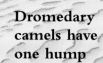

When they cannot find food, camels have been known to eat rope, sandals, and even tents!

Sloths don't clean their fur, so after a while green slime grows on it, and beetles and moths come to live in it!

WHY is a sloth so lazy?

Sloths spend most of their lives hanging upside down in trees in their **rain forest** habitat in South America. Sloths eat only the leaves of plants that grow nearby, so some days they hardly move more than an inch when looking for food. Staying still also helps them hide from their enemies.

Camels have thick coats to protect them from the heat of the sun. Pads on their feet help them walk on the hot sand. These pads also spread out—like snowshoes—helping them walk on loose sand.

Sidewinder snake

Now I know . . .

★ Mammals live in every part of the world—on land and in water.
★ Camels store fat in humps on their backs.
★ Sloths rarely move from their upside-down positions.

WHY are whales whoppers?

Larger than any dinosaur, the blue whale is the biggest animal that has ever lived. An adult can grow up to 108 feet (33m) long, the same length as a jumbo jet. It can weigh more than 150 tons, which is as heavy as 30 elephants. The blue whale is able to grow so huge because its giant body is always supported by the water around it. Whales are powerful swimmers. Some can even leap out of the water.

WHAT is a blowhole?

Aquatic mammals, such as whales and dolphins, cannot breathe underwater like fish. They must come to the surface for air. They breathe in and out through a **blowhole**. This is the nostril, or breathing hole, on the top of their heads. When they let out the used air, they release a spray of water called a spout.

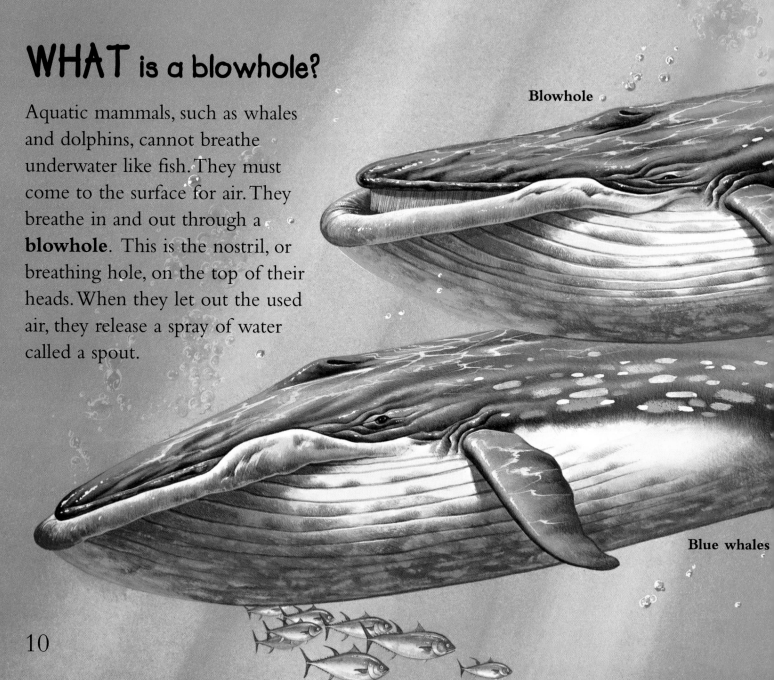

Blowhole

Blue whales

10

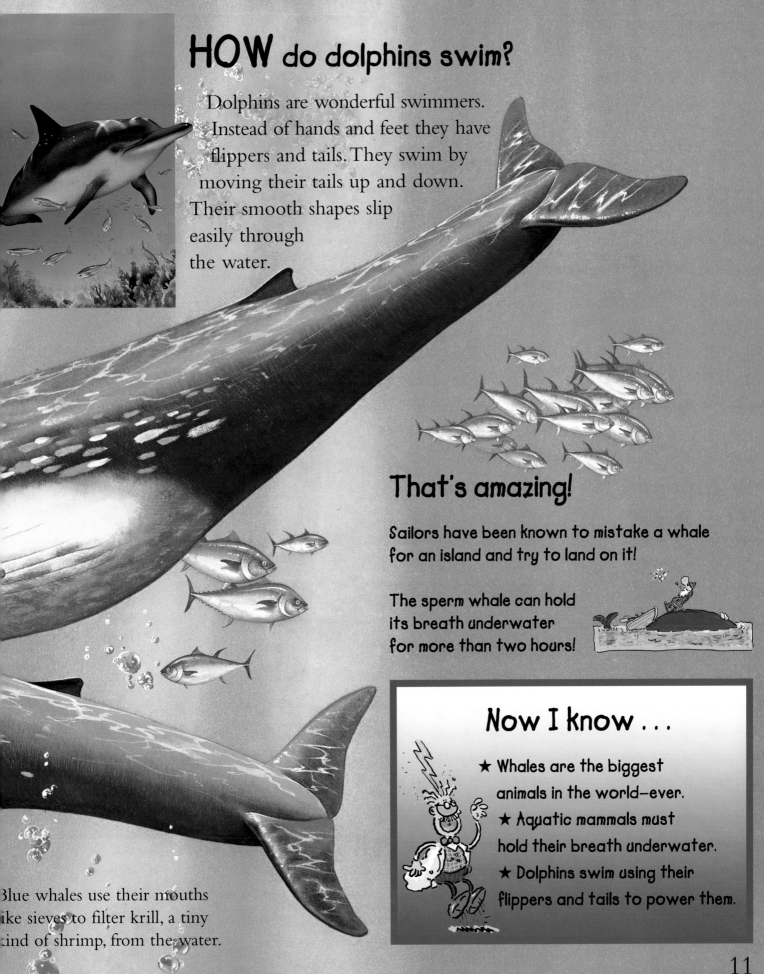

HOW do dolphins swim?

Dolphins are wonderful swimmers. Instead of hands and feet they have flippers and tails. They swim by moving their tails up and down. Their smooth shapes slip easily through the water.

That's amazing!

Sailors have been known to mistake a whale for an island and try to land on it!

The sperm whale can hold its breath underwater for more than two hours!

Now I know . . .

★ Whales are the biggest animals in the world—ever.
★ Aquatic mammals must hold their breath underwater.
★ Dolphins swim using their flippers and tails to power them.

Blue whales use their mouths like sieves to filter krill, a tiny kind of shrimp, from the water.

Look and find
★ caterpillar ★

WHICH mammals can fly?

Bats are the only mammals that truly fly. Like birds, they have light bodies, but they do not have feathers. Their wings are layers of skin stretched between long finger bones. Bats are **nocturnal**. They sleep during the day, hanging upside down from cave roofs or tree branches. As the sun sets, they fly into the night in search of food.

HOW do bats find food in the dark?

Most bats have poor sight. While hunting at night, they send out high-pitched squeaks that bounce off of objects and return to their ears as echoes. This is called **echolocation**. From these sounds, the bats can tell where things are—such as tasty insects.

Flying fox bat

Kitti's hog-nosed bat

This minute bat is one of the world's smallest mammals. It is about the size of a bumblebee and weighs around .07 ounces (2g).

That's amazing!

One type of insect-eating bat can eat 600 mosquitoes in one hour!

Sometimes millions of bats live together in a huge group called a colony!

12

WHY do sugar gliders leap from trees?

The Australian sugar glider leaps from the treetops to find food or to escape from its enemies. Although it does not have wings, it has a thin, furry skin that stretches along its body. This helps it glide from tree to tree. It can jump over 160 feet (50m).

Most bats are **insectivores**—they eat only insects. But some bats, such as the flying fox bat, eats the sweet nectar from fruits or flowers that open at night.

Now I know . . .

★ Bats have wings and are the only mammals that can fly like birds.
★ Sugar gliders cannot fly, but they do glide from tree to tree.
★ Most bats hunt during the night, using their excellent hearing.

WHAT do hippopotamuses eat?

Like many other mammals, the hippopotamus is a vegetarian and eats only plants. Plant-eating mammals are called **herbivores**. They have strong teeth to help them grind their tough food, and special stomachs to digest it. To get all the energy they need, they have to spend many hours every day feeding.

WHICH mammals chew and chew?

Hoofed mammals, such as buffaloes, giraffes, and antelopes, feed mainly on grass and leaves. Because their food is so tough, they chew their food twice. After grabbing a big mouthful, they quickly swallow it after one chew. The food goes into their stomachs, but comes back up for a second chew when it has become softer.

Elephants

Hippopotamus mother and baby

Buffaloes

Because they all eat a range of different foods, many herbivores can live in the same area. In the evening, when the sun has set, many herbivores go to the local water hole to eat.

A hippo bathing

14

Giraffes eating acacia leaves

WHY do giraffes have long necks and legs?

The world's tallest mammals are giraffes. They can be as tall as 16 feet (5m). They get their awesome height from their long necks and legs. Being so tall, giraffes can stretch right up into the trees and pull off juicy leaves and shoots that other animals cannot reach. Even though their necks are long, giraffes have only seven neck bones—the same number as all other mammals.

That's amazing!

As well as being the tallest mammal, a giraffe also has a huge tongue—more than 18 inches (45cm) long!

Hippos are very large animals—no wonder, they eat about 133 pounds (60kg) of plants every day!

antelope

Zebras drinking at a water hole

Some mammals, such as humans, can eat plants and meat. They are called **omnivores**.

Now I know . . .

★ Many mammals, such as hippos and giraffes, eat plants.

★ Some herbivores chew their food over and over again.

★ Giraffes have long necks and legs so they can reach treetops.

15

WHERE do lions catch their meals?

Mammals, such as lions, tigers, and cheetahs, that eat meat are called **carnivores**. Big cats are built to hunt. They have powerful bodies, sharp eyesight, and a good sense of smell. Lions live in family groups called **prides**. They hunt their **prey** on the plains and in the woodlands of Africa. The females of the group do most of the hunting, but the males soon arrive to make sure they get their share of the feast.

That's amazing!

Cheetahs make a lot of noises—they chirp, purr, hum, and yelp!

Tigers are strong swimmers. They take to the water to cross rivers, to go between islands, or just to cool down.

A lion can eat 50 pounds (23kg) of meat in one meal—that's the same as eating over 250 hamburgers!

16

WHAT is the fastest mammal?

The cheetah is the fastest mammal. It can run as fast as 68 miles per hour (110km/h), but only in short bursts. Unlike most cats, its claws stay out all the time, helping it grip the ground as it runs.

Two lionesses chase an antelope

WHY do tigers have stripes?

Tigers are easy to recognize, with thick black stripes covering their orange bodies. These markings help them blend in with the light and shade of the forest. They can creep up on their prey quickly and quietly without being noticed, especially at sunset, when they like to hunt.

Tiger

Now I know . . .

★ Carnivores, such as the big hunting cats, eat only meat.

★ The fastest mammal in the world is the speedy cheetah.

★ A tiger's stripes camouflage it in the forest.

17

HOW do beavers build their dams?

Many mammals build shelters to protect their young. A whole beaver family helps build a **dam** in the river. This structure is made from logs, branches, and rocks stuck together with mud. The beavers cut the logs by gnawing through trees with their sharp teeth. Inside the dam is an area above water that is warm and dry, even in bad weather. Here the beavers can raise their young in safety.

Beaver

WHY do dormice need a nest?

Dormice have nests to keep them snug and protected. During the cold winter, they spend several months asleep, or **hibernating**. The hibernating animal's body slows down, and its heart beats less often. It does not eat, but gets its energy from fat stored in its body.

That's amazing!

Beavers build canals more than 650 feet (200m) long to make quick routes from one river to another!

More than 400 million prairie dogs lived in one underground town in Texas!

WHERE do prairie dogs live?

A prairie dog is a type of rodent found in North America. Family groups dig underground burrows. These are linked together by tunnels, making "towns" for hundreds of prairie dogs. Some act as sentries and keep watch above ground for enemies.

Dam

Now I know . . .

★ Beavers live on rivers in wood dams, which are built by the whole family.
★ In the winter, hibernating animals keep warm in nests.
★ Prairie dogs live in burrows that link together, making towns.

19

Look and find butterfly

WHERE do gorillas live?

Gorillas are shy, gentle creatures that live in the remote forests of central Africa. They travel in family groups, which include an adult male, several females, and their babies. During the day a group will move slowly through the forest, looking for food and resting while the young play. Just before dark, the gorillas build their nests from branches and leaves and curl up to go to sleep.

WHO is the leader of the pack?

Wolves, like many other mammals, live in family groups. They hunt together in packs, which are led by a **dominant** male. When two wolves meet, they use body language to decide who is the boss.

Gray wolves in a pack

Silverback

That's amazing!

A baby gorilla will ride "piggyback" until it is almost three years old!

Despite what fairy tales say, wolves stay away from humans as much as possible!

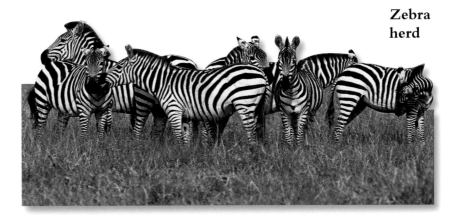

Zebra herd

WHY do zebras have stripes?

Zebras are famous for their stripes, but no one really knows why these African horses have them. It may be that the black-and-white pattern camouflages them. Or it may help keep zebras cool in the hot sun. Because no two zebras have exactly the same pattern, it is more likely that the stripes are like a signal, to help foals find their mothers in the large group.

Some male gorillas are called silverbacks. They get their name from the silver hairs that grow on their backs. These hairs appear when a male gorilla is about ten years old.

Now I know . . .

★ Gorillas live in family groups in the forests of central Africa.
★ Often groups of mammals are led by one male.
★ Zebras can tell each other apart by the stripes on their bodies.

WHEN do elephants stop growing?

When they are born, most mammal babies are blind and helpless, but newborn elephant calves can walk when they are just one hour old. Unlike other young, they never completely stop growing. The older they get, the larger they grow. Female elephants will stay with their mothers and relatives in the same herd long after they become adults.

HOW do young mammals learn?

Mammals give their young more protection and training than other animals do. Young mammals learn many skills from their mothers, such as finding food and staying out of danger. Sometimes the father also cares for the young. He protects them from predators and helps find food for them.

That's amazing!

When it is born, a baby elephant weighs 320 pounds (145kg)—over twice the weight of an adult human!

The Asian elephant is pregnant for 609 days—over two and half times as long as a human!

WHAT do piglets eat?

During their first few weeks a mother pig feeds her piglets on her milk. Mammals are the only animals that do this. Some mammals, such as elephants, feed milk to their young until they are several years old.

A young elephant is protected by the females in the herd

Elephants love bathing. They are very good swimmers and can give themselves a shower by squirting water through their trunks.

Now I know . . .

★ Elephants are so huge because they do not stop growing—ever.

★ Mammal mothers teach their babies survival skills.

★ Piglets, like all mammals, feed on their mother's milk.

23

WHAT does a kangaroo have in its pouch?

Kangaroos belong to a group of mammals called **marsupials**. Marsupial mothers have a pouch on the front of their bodies. When a baby kangaroo, or joey, is born, it is only about 0.8 inches (2cm) long. It is too tiny to survive on its own, so it crawls into its mother's warm pouch. Once safely inside the baby drinks its mother's milk and continues to grow. After eight months, it is big enough to live outside.

Like most marsupials kangaroos are only found in the wild in Australia.

That's amazing!

The leaves that koala bears eat contain strong-smelling oils that act as a bug repellent!

A platypus finds food in the mud, using special electric sensors inside its bill!

Female red kangaroo with her joey

WHY do koalas have to sleep all the time?

Koalas live in the treetops, eating the leaves and young shoots of a particular tree —the eucalyptus. Their leafy diet does not give them a lot of energy, so they spend up to 18 hours a day asleep. They only become active at night, when it is time to eat again.

WHICH mammals lay leathery eggs?

Two mammals, the platypus and the echidna, a spiny anteater, do not give birth to live young. Instead they lay eggs, which are protected by leathery shells. After laying her eggs in a nest, the mother platypus warms them with her body for about 10 days until they hatch. Mammals that lay eggs are called **monotremes**.

Now I know . . .

★ A female kangaroo has a pouch so that her baby has a safe place to grow.

★ Koalas are lazy—they sleep for up to 18 hours every day.

★ The platypus and the echidna are the only mammals that lay eggs.

25

WHY do chimps chatter?

Almost all mammals have some way of **communicating** with animals of their own kind. Chimpanzees communicate, or "chatter," using sounds and signs. They bark, pant, or grunt to tell others when food has been found. They hoot loudly and beat on tree trunks to warn when enemies are nearby. Chimps often greet each other with hugs and kisses, just like humans.

That's amazing!

Scientists have found that chimps treat themselves for illnesses using plants from the forest as medicine!

Wild chimps use leaves as sponges to soak up water or to drink!

Young chimpanzee

WHAT does a dog's bark mean?

Dogs bark at other animals to tell them where their **territory** is. An animal's territory is the area that it moves around in and where it feeds. A pet dog's territory may be around its owner's house. Dogs will also bark if they are excited or just want to say "hello."

Sheep dog

WHICH mammals love to "talk"?

Like other intelligent mammals, dolphins are playful and communicative. They live in groups called schools and "talk" to each other using clicks and whistles. These sounds travel under the water for many miles. Scientists also think dolphins can copy human speech, but at a much faster rate.

A chimp communicates with its group

Chimps spend a lot of time in trees. They use their strong arms to swing from branch to branch, looking for food. At night, they build treetop nests from leaves and sleep in them.

Now I know . . .

★ Chimps send messages to each other using sounds and signs.

★ A dog's bark can mean "hello" or "keep away, please!"

★ Dolphins are intelligent and "talk" to each other.

WHY are tigers in danger?

The tiger is one of the most **endangered** animals in the wild. For many years, thousands have been killed illegally by hunters for their fur and other body parts. In Asia, farmers have cut down the tigers' forest home to grow crops. To help these animals survive, special areas called **reserves** have been created for them, where hunting is banned. Many zoos have tried to breed tigers to release back into the wild.

WHO hunts rhinoceroses?

In Asia, illegal hunters, called poachers, kill thousands of rhinoceroses for their horns every year. The horns are ground up and used in medicine because many people believe they can cure illnesses. Because of hunting, rhinos are the fastest-disappearing large mammals in the world.

White rhinoceros

That's Amazing!

A tiger's mighty roar can be heard over 2 miles (3km) away!

ROAR

Rhino horn is made from keratin—the same material that your hair and nails are made from!

HOW many pandas are left in the wild?

Fewer than 1,000 wild pandas still live in their natural home in the mountain forests of southern China. So few are left because they feed on a plant called bamboo, which is becoming rare in this area. Another problem is that pandas have only a few babies in their lifetime, and many of them die young.

Mammals that live in the ocean are in danger of dying out, too. Although most whales and dolphins are protected, many of them are killed every year.

Now I know...

★ Tigers are becoming rare—reserves are being set up to protect them.

★ Rhinos are hunted by poachers for their valuable horns.

★ Pandas are very rare. Fewer than 1,000 are left in the wild.

MAMMAL QUIZ

What have you remembered about mammals? Test what you know and see how much you have learned.

1 What does a giant panda eat?
a)   Bamboo
b)   Grass
c)   Eucalyptus

2 Which mammal has blubber?
a)   Mouse
b)   Gorilla
c)   Walrus

3 Which mammal eats only plants?
a)   Giraffe
b)   Lion
c)   Polar bear

4 Which mammal lives in a dam?
a)   Dolphin
b)   Koala
c)   Beaver

5 Which mammal has a pouch?
a)   Seal
b)   Bat
c)   Koala

6 Which mammal can fly?
a)   Sugar glider
b)   Bat
c)   Kangaroo

7 Which mammal is the fastest runner?
a)   Bat
b)   Whale
c)   Cheetah

8 What sound does a dolphin make?
a)   Whistle
b)   Bark
c)   Roar

9 What is a camel's hump made of?
a)   Blubber
b)   Hair
c)   Fat

10 Where does a polar bear live?
a   Desert
b)   Arctic
c)   Jungle

Find the answers on page 32.

GLOSSARY

arctic The cold area around the North Pole.

blowhole The nostrils of a whale or dolphin, found on the top of the head.

blubber A thick layer of fat under an aquatic mammal's skin, which keeps it warm.

camouflage A color, shape, or pattern that hides something. A camouflaged animal looks just like its background, so it is hard to see.

carnivores Animals that eat mainly meat.

communicating The passing on of information, feelings, and ideas.

dam A beaver's home, built from logs and rocks stuck together with mud.

den The hollowed out home of a wild animal.

dominant The most powerful animal in a group.

echolocation A navigation system used by bats and dolphins to find their way in the dark.

endangered When a species is at risk of dying out.

habitat The natural home of an animal or plant.

herbivores Animals that eat only plants.

hibernation When animals spend the winter months in a deep sleep.

insectivores Animals that only eat insects.

marsupials Mammals, such as kangaroos and koalas, that raise their young in pouches.

monotremes Mammals that lays eggs rather than giving birth to live young.

nocturnal Animals that are busy and active at night and a sleep during the day.

omnivores Animals that eat both meat and plants.

prey An animal that is hunted or killed by another animal.

prides Family groups of lions.

rain forest A dense forest with very heavy rainfall.

reserves Special areas where wild animals are protected from poachers and the land is free from farming.

rodents Small mammals with large, sharp front teeth for gnawing.

species A particular type of animal or plant.

territory The area in which an animal lives and hunts.

warm-blooded Having a constant body temperature.

INDEX

Answers to the Mammals Quiz on page 30

★ 1 a ★ 2 c ★ 3 a ★ 4 c ★ 5 c ★ 6 b ★ 7 c ★ 8 a ★ 9 c ★ 10 b